AF365272

VISCOUS PROPERTY OF EPIDERMAL MUCOUS CELLS OF BURROWING SNAKE EEL – A HISTOCHEMICAL ANALYSIS

Editor

Dr. K. Jayalakshmi

Department of Zoology, Tagore Government Arts and Science College, Puducherry, India.

Published by

JPS Scientific Publications
India

Published by

JPS Scientific Publications, Tamil Nadu, India.
E.mail: jpsscientificpublications@gmail.com
Website: www.jpsscientificpublications@gmail.com

Published in India.

International Standard Book Number (ISBN): 978-81-935636-2-5

Learn to read

Read the words

The **ant** is red.

My **bag** is pink.

The **can** is empty.

The **doll** is pretty.

I bought two **eggs**.

Read the words

 My **fan** is colorful.

 **God** is kind.

 I have a simple **home**.

 The **ice** is melting.

 I bought a jar of **jam**.

Read the words

 The **king** is noble.

 The **lady** is dancing.

 I drink **milk** everyday.

 The **nurse** is working.

 The **owl** has big eyes.

Read the words

I ate **pizza** yesterday.

The **queen** is graceful.

Daddy gave me a **ring**.

The bath **soap** is fragrant.

I want to **ride** a train.

Joan has an **umbrella**.

She plays the **violin**.

The man found his **wallet**.

The **xerox** machine is rusty.

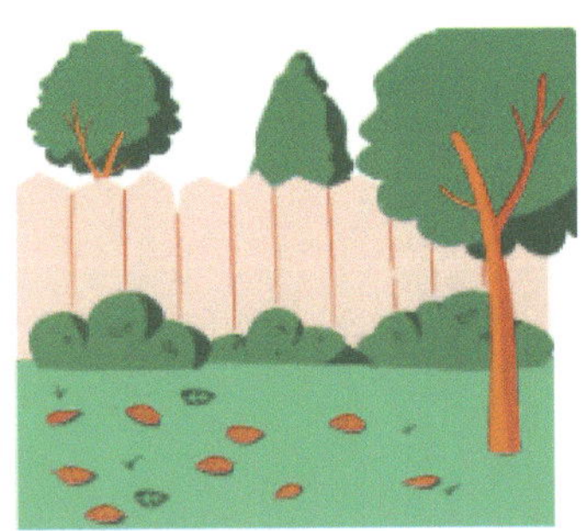

The back **yard** is dirty.

Children love the **zoo.**

Learn
to read
and
rhyme!

- Apple

A is for Apple
Red and healthy
Biting sweetly
For snack and pastry.

- Baby

B is for Baby
Just like you and me
Please don't worry
I'm just cute and wee.

Read and rhyme

- Cat

C is for Cat
Sleepy and quiet
Wait till their paws hit
Oh so tireless a pet!

Dog

D is for Dog
Friendly and playful
They run, they roll
Waits for you after school.

Eggplant

**E is for Eggplant
Shiningly purpled
Cooked, fried, and boiled
It tastes very good.**

Friend

**F is for Friend
You will meet them
dearest brethren
Funny as a cartoon.**

- Gold

G is for Gold
Sparkling and sweet
When you win in a feast
It's the prize you collect

- Happy

H is for Happy
And no words can say
How happy I'll be
When you smile at me.

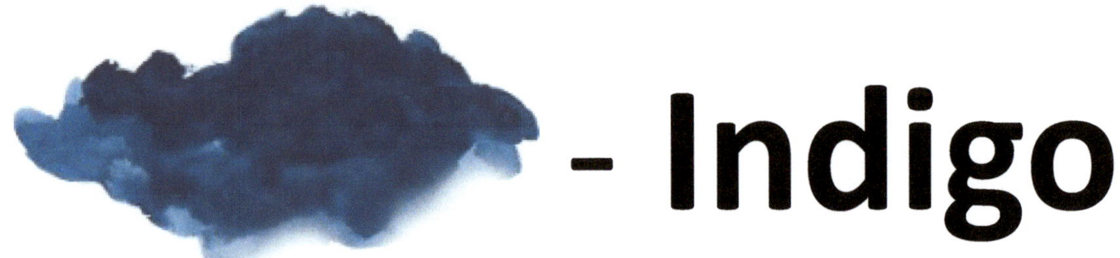

- Indigo

**I is for Indigo
A color hard to view
But when you try once more
It's a part of the rainbow.**

- Juice

**J is for Juice
From fruits so sweet
Squeeze it and pour it
In your glass to drink.**

- Kite

K is for Kite
carried by the gust
One day we'll play it
Summer is not over yet.

. Love

L is for Love
My love for Mom and Dad
The reason why I'm glad
Everyday of my life.

 **- Mommy**

**M is for Mommy
Who always beside me
Keeping me happy
Strong, cute, and healthy.**

 **- Numbers**

**N is for Numbers
Let's try to discover
How to count together
Start counting all over..**

 - # Niña

**Ñ is for niño and niña
Two babies in a villa
Sharing a good aura
Wake up, wait for Santa.**

 - # Ninong

**Ng is for *ninang* and *ninong*
In Christmas season
We will jump with joy
We'll buy candies and toys.**

Note Ninong/Ninang - Godparents

- Oranges

O is for Oranges
It tastes so sweet
Eat or drink its juices
You'll surely enjoy it.

- Puppy

P is for a Puppy
So cute and funny
Playful and friendly
Tireless or sleepy.

 **- Queen**

**Q is for the Queen
In her royal throne
Graceful and beautiful
Like daisy in a bloom.**

 **- Reading**

**R is for Reading
You'll love and not tiring
To find many things
Learning is exciting.**

Stars

S is for Stars
Above the clouds
In heaven they are dots
Seen during the nights.

Trombone

T is for Trombone
That plays in parading
Tralalala, keep singing
And happily marching.

Umbrella

**U is for Umbrella
In rainy days, a charm
Keeping us dry and warm
It comforts 'till dawn.**

- Violin

**V is for Violin
Its nice tune
Can make you whine
Play it nice and fine.**

Walrus

W is for Walrus
We see them in fine day
They are cute and gay
With teeth so funny.

Xylophone

X is for Xylophone
Another melody in tune
Do re mi fa sol
Repeat it once more.

- Yes

Y is for saying YES
You're blessed everyday
Y is for saying yes
Everyone's doing okay.

'ipper

Z is for Zipper
Close and open
You keep it loosen
Sometimes its tighten.

COPYRIGHT © HAVE FUN WITH WORDS
By ROY BASA and ROZEL BASA

ISBN
Hardbound-978-621-470-348-7
Softbound/Paperback-978-621-470-349-4
MOBI/KINDLE-978-621-470-350-0

Published by:
Poetry Planet Book Publishing House
Rosario, Pozorrubio, Pangasinan, Philippines
Contact No.: 09554960044
Email: maritesritumalta@gmail.co

ROY B. BASA
LPT, PhD, DHum, DMin, DSc, FPOd, FRIEdr

Roy Basa was born and raised in Murcia, Negros Occidental, Philippines by Raul and Lilia Basa together with his other 6 siblings. He graduated his elementary education from Lopez Jaena Elementary School.

He then went to La Consolacion College, Murcia for his secondary education where he graduated as Class Valedictorian. He got his Bachelor's in Education major in General Science, Master's in School Administration and Supervision, and Doctor of Philosophy major in Educational Management at the University of Negros Occidental – Recoletos where he graduated with Outstanding Dissertation and High Academic Distinction Awards. He then took another masterate, the Master in Natural Science at the University of St. La Salle, Bacolod under a scholarship grant, Project – Free Paglaum.

He was a high school, college, and graduate school science teacher for 18 years in the Philippines and 3 years as a high school science teacher in Arizona and New Mexico, USA, respectively.

He was awarded as one of the Most Outstanding Teachers of the Philippines in 2016 by the Metrobank Foundation, Philippines. Recently, he was also awarded by Asia – Pacific Luminare Awards as "Asia's Most Remarkable and Exceptional Science and CTE Educator of the Year 2022.

ROZEL JAENA BASA, MBA

Rozel Jaena Basa was born in Bacolod City and raised in Murcia, Negros Occidental, Philippines by Romeo and Razel Jaena together with her other 3 siblings. She graduated with her elementary education from Murcia Elementary School. She then went to La Consolacion College, Murcia for her secondary education. She got her Bachelor of Science in Information Management and Master's in Business Administration at the University of Negros Occidental – Recoletos

She was a former Manager at Golden Sun Finance Corporation, Bacolod City, Philippines for 16 years. Recently, she is one of the Educational Assistants for Pre – K to 2 at Shiwi Ts'ana Elementary School, Zuni, New Mexico, USA.